Mireille ZAMBEAU

Save-me!

or

Kill-me!

Diary of a misunderstood teenager

Save-me or Kill-me! by Mireille Zambeau
Code ISBN: 9798401770516

Translated from French:
Valerie Adefokun / Charazad Abderrahmani

To my little sister Nathalie F.
& Marie-Claude my adopted mother,
my oxygen.

1.

Bitterness

«Dear parents,

I wanted to call you Thursday night, but...

End of November 1982...

My name is Christine Sogera; I'm sixteen years old. My teenage life is complicated like that of all young girls my age who are looking for themselves.

Alone, in my bedroom, I'm facing my desk; night has already fallen. It was very cold today; it was a gloomy day, both for the weather and for my life as a high school student.

We are in France, a small Moselle village, Corny-sur-Moselle, lost in the middle of nowhere, counting 1248 souls; there is not much to do when you are between thirteen and eighteen except just hanging out and chatting with friends in front of the church or watching the boys from FC Noveant train on the football field. For my part, like every evening, after preparing the family meal and washing the dishes, I do my never-ending homework.

I love this moment when I find myself alone, quiet, without the incessant noise caused by my five-year-old little sister Marie, who moans all the time and steals my things. Still, she's adorable with her shoulder-length blonde curls and pretty cheeky blue eyes; mom says she is my spitting image when I was little. But I don't know if I was as energetic as Marie, a real little neutron.

I asked her to be nice and to leave me alone. I think my mom is going to bed soon. So, I'm busy reading my school agenda and starting to think about my essay due in two days.

Alas, barely ten minutes later, my little sister shows up in my room without asking permission, takes a sheet of paper from my desk, my fountain pen and scribbles letters. Without success, I ask her to leave; she hums knowing that it stresses me. I can't concentrate because I had a bad day in high school, the tension mounts, I repeat my request for my sister to come out of my room, I raise my voice.

Gesticulating near me, Marie bumps into my tea mug on the desk, which spills over on my school supplies. It is too much, I see red, I hit her for the first time and especially without thinking about the consequences which are not long in arriving. Marie screams as if I had cut off her finger.

Mom, already into her purple dressing gown, a floral scarf around her head, to preserve her brushing for the next day, storms into my room and seeing the mark of my fingers on Marie's cheek, slaps me.

I'm speechless, my wet eyes turned to my mother. I look at her in silence. She never hit me so hard, a tear runs down my cheek, I'm sad and shocked, shocked that she doesn't understand that I need quiet time for myself, shocked by that slap I did not see happen.

At this moment, everything jostles in my head, Marie glued to my mother leaves the room and even adds a little more, to attract her attention.

Moments with my mother? I no longer have them anymore. My father always on the road, only comes home on weekends. I manage everything, meals, cleaning, my little sister. It's not fair, why? My sight is blurred, I burst into tears; I'm alone and with no one to hug me. I feel misunderstood, totally abandoned, desperate... My eyes are filled with tears; I try to concentrate on my essay, but I can't finish it, it's a pointless effort. My thoughts are so negative after this violent slap that it prevents me from thinking.

Later, I go to bed silently, wanting to be alone and being very upset. I can't sleep or ignore what happened. Subconsciously, I hope that my mother comes knocking on my bedroom door to chat with me, to explain, to apologize, to kiss me, to reassure me. But nothing happens, it's total silence everything's is still and quiet. Psychologically exhausted, I fall asleep.

The next morning, I wake up late, didn't hear my alarm clock, and my mom didn't call me. Why? Everything is calm in the house, Mum is not there, neither is Marie. Given the time, surely, she already dropped her off at kindergarten. I prepare in a hurry, grab an apple from the fruit basket as I walk by and run to take the ten o'clock bus, the one that brings the locals into town, my school bus only comes very early in the morning, it's not easy to live in the countryside. I look at the clock; I'm over an hour and a half late, I'm sure I'll be in detention. Too bad!

When I arrive-at the Jean Moulin Sixth form School in *Metz*[1], I go through the supervisors' office and as I expect, I have an hour of detention for the same evening. I explain that this is not possible, that I have to pick up my little sister from the evening daycare. The supervisor replies: "*We are going to tell your mother, who will work it out*"; she hands me my correspondence notebook[2], and orders me to go to class.

The day went by without too many pitfalls, if I do not take into account Graciela the madwoman, a first-year student who believes herself superior to all, like an offspring who comes from a wealthy family and who, despite

---

[1] City located in the east of France
[2] Contact book between parent-teacher

everything, does not hesitate to harass, hit and even extort other people.

Back home, after my hour of detention, I notice that my mother has picked up my little sister from school and she looks very upset. No doubt she was forced to quit her job earlier. Mom is busy in the kitchen and doesn't say a word. I don't dare approach her to kiss her, lest she pushes me away. I wouldn't stand it. I throw her a:

— Hi, did you have a good day?

No answer... Marie stays in her corner without talking to me too, or even looking at me. Sad, I go up to my room and lock myself there.

It's time for dinner, I'm not going downstairs and my mom is not calling me. I feel really bad. How can she ignore me so much?

So, what is this message she's trying to get to me? It's my turn to be upset and I go to bed with an empty belly.

Then my negative thoughts come back again, she doesn't love me, she would be happier if I wasn't there. As for my father, let's not talk about it; and he's never here anyway and the weekend is never available for me, he spends more time with his soccer buddies.

The more I ruminate, the more I cry. Suddenly I have a revelation; I get up, and stuff some things and my savings into my gym bag.

My decision is made, tomorrow I will leave my family forever, without regret. They will only get what they want, peace. It is ten-thirty pm, I fall asleep, my eyes wet with tears.

2.

Misery

The next day, I get up looking puffy from the day before. I'm getting ready for high school after a quick breakfast. Without worrying about my mother's gaze, I walk to the front door, grab my backpack, my gym bag, and walk out.

At the same time, my mother asks me:

— Do you have any sport today?

Without a word to her, I walk through the door and keep walking. My mother, coming closer to the front door, yells nastily at me:

— Oh! I'm talking to you, Christine, come back here now! I'll teach you politeness, she yells.

I don't answer and continue on my way. She screams at me:

— Watch out for your tonight, when you come back!

Without looking back, ignoring her screams, not understanding why she is so angry with me, I hurried away, tears streaming down my cheeks without stopping.

Arriving at the bus stop, I meet my great friend from high school Valerie. She is so pretty from her five-feet tall frame and her long straight blonde hair, falling down to her lower back and brown eyes. I love her hippie style. Zen and fun, that's exactly what I need this morning, she notices my sad face. She asks me what's happening to me. Before telling her my intention to run away, I make her promise to keep a secret.

The promise made, I tell her about everything that happened regarding the slap in every detail possible, but also that my house has become hell, that I do everything at home, that I don't have time for myself. I can understand that it is not easy for my mother to manage my little sister and me, because she works a lot, my father is absent during the week professionally and we are often alone with her. I noticed that my parents didn't get along too well anymore. Every now and then, being on the road during the week, my dad calls my mom and I hear her scream, then cry. It's really not easy at home right now.

I admit to Valerie that I don't want to go home anymore, that I have packed my things and brought some money. My decision is well thought and well made, whatever she may tell me. She understands me, but tries to talk me out of it. We continue our journey in the bus without talking about it; I notice that Valerie is worried and sad, but she promised not to say anything and I trust her.

Once at school, Valerie and I meet three classmates who notice my red eyes and my gym bag.

— Hey beauty, what's happening to you? Why do you have your gym bag, we don't have sport today, said the first girl.

— I know !

— But what do you have? she retorts.

— Nothing at all! I say coldly to close the discussion.

— They turn to Valerie, hoping for answers, I glare at her, she remains silent. We all go back to class. At noon, in the refectory, one of my friends, curious, approaches me and informs me that Valerie has explained my problem to her and what I intend to do. I'm furious with Valerie, and Sophie notices It. She explains to me that she and Valerie are worried about me and want to help me. They don't approve of what I'm about to do and think I'll regret it later.

Despite their words, I don't change my mind; I want to prove to them that I can do it and to show my parents that I don't need them. My dismay is too strong. I'm sick of being told what to do, I don't need anyone.

I shout at Sophie while turning on my heels, very angry:

— Leave me alone!

In the afternoon, during Miss Doubs's literature class, she notices that I'm the only one with a sports bag. She asks me to come to her desk and quietly tells me:

— Why do you have your sports bag, there is no sport lesson today, it seems to me?

Having I feel like I've been caught in the act, I answer her as calmly as possible:

— Yes, I know, tonight, I will be sleeping at my grandparents, because my mother is away for two days.

— Okay, fine, go sit down, she said to

me at last.

In my head, I breathe a light sigh of relief, proud that I got out of it so easily, despite this little lie.

Finally, I find her sympathetic, despite her structured bun above her head, her long black straight skirt and her gray cardigan fitted to her waist. She wants to appear strict to get the upper hand because I think she is very young.

At the end of class, my friends turn away from me and frown on me. I know very well why they are so quiet, but whatever, my decision is made.

I've been thinking about it all day, where could I go to run away? I make a plan, change my mind, then it's enlightenment: as soon as I leave high school, head to Metz station and take the first train to Paris. My plan looks great, I'm happy to start this adventure and the adrenaline rushes through my body, I feel better.

At the end of class, I leave high school alone, without a word or a glance for my friends. Lost in my thoughts and almost happy, a voice calls out to me:

— Christine!!! Do you want me to drop you off at your grandparents? Come !

— No thank you Miss Doubs, I'm going to take the bus, you are very kind, I do not want to disturb you.

— But you don't bother me, come on, come on, it's better to have company when we travel, she said with a broad smile.

I'm trapped, so I get into my teacher's car, hugging my bags, and trying to quickly think of a fallback. Before starting, she asks me for my grandparents' address, which is a problem for me because I don't know what to say to her. In my head, I say to myself: "*think, think.... Quick*". Her voice brings me out of my lethargy and my thinking.

— Christine, I'm listening to you!!

I mumble :

— Uh!!! Sorry, yes 27, Town Hall Square in Jouy-aux-Arches, uh!!! No sorry, 56 School Street... Oh, please leave me, I don't want you to take me away.

I get out of the car in a hurry and run down the street, straight ahead, without looking back, as if I had a stranger chasing me. My heart is pounding; I find it hard to catch my breath. I don't know what my teacher is thinking, and if she is following me, but I run, I run quickly.

After a while, I stopped in the corner to hide, I try to calm myself down, and slowly catch my breath. I look right and left to see if someone has followed me and I can't see anyone. I wait a little longer to be sure and I finally leave for Metz station.

I take a few francs out of my wallet, I go to the main counter, and with my best smile, I ask for a ticket for the next train to Paris. An emotion rises in me, shared between the joy and the fear of this adventure so close.

3.

Freedom

Sitting in the *Corail*[3] train, I'm exhilarated, it is 5.40 pm and the train leaves. I look out the window, no policeman in sight looking for me. I imagine my mother warned them! Or maybe she didn't notice my absence. And that the daycare had to call her to pick up my little sister.

---

[3] Name given to an SNCF passengers rail car in 1975

At this moment, I don't care because I feel free, finally free! I see the stations passing by, one by one, while eating the tuna sandwich I bought before getting on the train. The night has fallen since longtime, it's a little cold, I don't understand, yet the train is heated. I believe it's the stress of the last two days.

So, I tighten my scarf against me and fall asleep

I wake up with a start, the Police officer? No, just a nice smiling train' controller who wakes me up and tells me that we have arrived at Paris East Railway Station. I thank him, get up and get out of the train. I discovered this big station and remember having come there with my parents a long time ago, well before the birth of my little sister Marie. A rush of emotion fills me with sadness, as I can see myself holding my parents' hand on either side.

I have to think about where I'm going to sleep; it's extremely late, 10.30 pm. I admit to being a little confused, tired. I sit on a bench in the station and try to clear my mind. Being in my thoughts, I do not see a group of young people who advance towards me laughing. There are three boys and two girls. I find them nice and start a discussion with them.

— Hi, are you lost? We've been watching you for a while now, do you need help? A girl in her twenties, a cigarette in her mouth, says to me with a hint of Italian accent in her voice.

— Hi, lost, yes and no, in fact, I came to Paris on a whim and I admit not having thought of where to sleep tonight.

— Did you run away from home? asks a youth of the gang, already knowing the obviousness of my answer.

So, I decide not to lie and just nod. He looks around at his friends and says to me.

— Hi, I'm Eric; this is Corinne, Sandra, Freddie and Patrick. If you want, you can come with us, we have a squat near the North Station, it's not very far.

I give him a smile and accept this great proposal. We all go together towards the exit of the station. I'm relieved.

At the same time, anguish rises in Corny-sur-Moselle

— I don't understand, my mother said over the phone. She still hasn't come home, I went to meet her best friends, I called their parents, and they don't know anything. Everyone told me that she went to class this morning. Tomorrow, I'll see with the school, now it's closed. Listen James, come home, please, I'm too scared. Do you think I should call the police?

— Of course, you have to, he said.

— Okay, I'll call them right away. I told my parents to come to get Marie, declared my mother between two sobs. I'm extremely worried, And it's cold very outside. I hope nothing has happened to her; she cries.

Paris - North Station district

My first night of freedom is great This group of young people is great, we laugh, we tell each other incredible things, yet we don't really know each other. I smoke my first joint and I feel good, so relaxed, I think her that's how life should be and I fall

31

asleep peacefully against Eric. He has brown hair and bottle green eyes; I think he looks a bit like *Yves Duteil*[4]. We often played this game of similarities with mom, well, that was before. He came closer to me to keep me warm, which is very kind of him.

The next day, we hang out in the neighborhood, and then we go around in the tube begging. I have some money left, but I keep it just in case, at the bottom of my gym bag. I follow the group without flinching; it's already nice that they accept me. I'm starting to know them a little, apart from the naughty little brown hair Sandra who is seventeen; they are all of legal age.

After two days of hanging out in Paris with my new friends and the euphoria of

---

[4] French singer-songwriter

the beginning fading away, I realize that I miss my heated bedroom a bit. I'm cold, I'm hungry, but I said nothing, we nibbled a little while sharing what we bought with the money from begging. I notice that Corinne and Patrick are together as well as Sandra and Freddie. I understand better why Eric is getting closer to me I feel good with them, it's reassuring!

In the meanwhile, at the High School Jean Moulin in Metz

— No, but I think I'm dreaming, my father yells in the principal's office where Miss Doubs livid tells him he facts of our last interview.

— I'm sorry Mister Sogera, I didn't imagine Christine was planning a runaway, she cries. She told me she was going to her grandparents, and...

— You are just an ignorant one, my

33

father cuts violently. And we pay you to take care of our children, you are just an idiot. I warn you that if anything happens to my daughter, I will hold you solely responsible.

With these few outbursts of rage, leaves the principal's office, slamming the door. He joins my mother at home and ends his rage on her.

Paris

I've been squatting with them for six nights, we have a good laugh, it's really nice, except that Eric sticks to me a little too much for my taste and it bothers me more and more. It's true that it's cold at night, we're a little stoned by drugs, I don't dare push him away too much, because I'm afraid of his reaction and of being alone in Paris. I'm really not comfortable with him.

I'm trying to talk to Sandra about it, because she's almost my age. However, not being really my friend, she is not receptive and does not understand why this can bother me so much, and says:

— Eric is a handsome brown 'hair with green eyes, he's super cute, don't you think? If I were you, I would jump at the chance!

But I am not her, so I try to figure this out on my own.

Two nights later Eric comes up to me and tries to kiss me, I'm a little too relaxed because I smoke more and more cannabis with them and I admit that alcohol keeps me hot in the cold of December. So, I give in to his kisses, but without really wanting it, I just have a great need for tenderness.

Alas, all of a sudden, his hand moves

tenderly over my body, then it becomes more pressing, on parts where no one has ever dared to put their hand. I'm dazed, but I know what I don't want and at first, I gently push his hand away, saying "No", but he insists; I shout another "NO" at him while pushing him violently. And there, everything happens so fast; he tears my clothes, he blocks my face against the ground, I struggle. He digs his fingers into my teenage body, He has no right, I suffer, I scream, cry, but nothing helps, he is brutal, takes me savagely by force and abuses me for a long time, too long. It's too late, I get raped, I have no more energy, like a larva, I don't move and I end up letting go. I really didn't expect this for my first time. Why is this happening to me? I hate myself so much. Do I deserve it? Is it my fault that I let myself be kissed? *"Oh, my God, I feel so dirty"*. I try to struggle, but he continues, gasps, gives little hoarse cries. After a moment, which I find interminable, he finishes his business, finally withdraws from me and turns his back on me.

I try somehow to get dressed, pulling my clothes up on me, but I stay prostrate in my corner, crying all the time. I'm so ashamed of myself. Why don't I have any support from others? Why has no one helped me? I hate myself; I want to vomit, but also to die!!!!

The next day I don't talk to Eric anymore, I'm too angry and ashamed of him and me. He approaches me, apologizes, and tells me that I'm beautiful, that he was under the influence of drugs and alcohol, so I wouldn't to blame him, that he loves me… I don't believe it at all! I'm lost and I really don't want to be alone in Paris, or to go back to my parents. So, I stupidly forgive Eric. The course of our life of debauchery resumes.

After another day of begging passers-by and nightfall, we walk towards the squat talking loudly. And there, fury, a police raid; they are in the squat and call out to us when we arrive. In a hurry, everyone runs, we separate to give the police a hard time. I run away, I hide, I'm scared... After a while, I realize that I don't have my gym bag with me, it stayed in the squat with my savings in it.

The alert on my disappearance has surely been issued; I've been wandering around Paris for almost two weeks. Now that I am alone, I have lost the group that so kindly greeted me when I arrived. In any case, I don't regret Eric for his violent behaviour. I'm cold! I try to return to the squat to retrieve my bag, but we can no longer access it, it has been padlocked by the police. Eric and the others are nowhere to be found. At night, I sleep in the street or if I'm lucky, inside a building or in a laundromat. I beg during the day to be able to eat, I am dirty and I am hungry. But going home is out of the question. I'm too ashamed and above all, I know what to expect, my mother told me as she left. I feel so much pain when I think about all of this. Moreover, it is true that it is easier to leave than to find the courage to come back.

Meanwhile in Metz, my friends are being questioned by the police

Valerie breaks down and cries with anguish not to hear from me and tells what she knows, but not about where I might have been, and for good reason, I haven't told her anything.

The investigations continue unabated. The surveillance videos show that I went to Metz station. The police officers are therefore expanding their research outside the city.

4.

Uncertainties

Paris

The tube took me to Republic Square. I ended up leaving the North Station district because it scares me, there are a lot of drug addicts and I'm not at ease there. I wander and head for streets behind, trying to find a quiet spot.

To warm up as best I can, I spend one more night in a building entrance at

20, Léon Jouhaux Road. I remember that we talked about this character at the High school of Metz in literature class. "*Mister Léon Jouhaux, a revolutionary trade unionist Libertarian and Nobel Peace Prize in 1951*". I don't know why it stuck in my mind.

A slender woman in her fifties, bundled up in her beige cashmere coat, a scarf pulled up to her nose and a brown beanie pulled over her head, walks into the building with me. She looks me from head to toe, pouted at my deplorable state, then turns to her mailbox. She checks if there is mail, turns to me a second time and says in a soft and reassuring voice:

— Are you hungry?

Surprised that she is speaking to me and exhausted by the situation I find myself in right now, I say to her very quietly:

— A little, but it will be fine, thank you very much Madam.

— Come on home, don't be afraid. You are going to eat and I can run a bath for you, it will warm you up.

In the face of such generosity, I follow her. Tears bead on my cheeks.

After climbing two floors on foot, I arrive in a very warm interior, a Christmas tree already sits in the living room. It reminds me of Marie who adored decorating it with me. A lump is swelling in my throat.

Everything is furnished with a lot of taste; I feel a little ashamed to be there. This woman so well dressed who reached out to me, a homeless stranger.

— Do you want to take a bath while I prepare the meal? I'm going to run you a bath and provide you with clean clothes that belonged to my daughter, it's about your size I think, she tells me.

— Your daughter doesn't live here anymore?

— Seeing her face darken, I immediately regret asking.

— Come on, the bathroom is over here, she said without answering my question.

The sound of the water filling the tub soothes me. I hear the lady humming in the kitchen busy preparing the meal, I think to myself that really lucky to have met her. I undress, enter the tub gently. Hot water surrounds my aching body from the last contractions of the winter cold. "*May it make me feel good*", I close my eyes and relax. I feel like I'm in another world.

After thirty minutes, maybe more, I walk through the kitchen door in her daughter's clean, warm clothes. The meal in preparation smells really great, the woman smiles at me and offers me a hot cup of tea. "*The meal is almost ready*", she tells me. I thank her again for everything she does for me.

She turns to me, smiles again and says:

— I'm happy you're here Veronique, it's been so long.

— My name is Christine, I told her very softly for fear of rushing her.

— Excuse-me, Veronique is my daughter's first name, because of the clothes, I got lost. Sorry Christine, I'm confused. My name is Marie-Claude,

Marie-Claude Blin.

— Don't worry Mrs. Blin, it does not matter, I said, thank you again for this nice hot bath, these clothes and this future meal, I don't want to disturb you. I admit I feel a lot better now.

— You don't disturb me; I live alone and that gives me company. It's almost Christmas, it's good to do a good deed. If you want, you can sleep here, your room is always free my darling. So, tell me how did you get there.

I jump a little when I hear her say the phrase: "*Your bedroom is still free my darling*", I'm afraid but I say nothing, I probably misheard.

While enjoying her succulent homemade vegetable soup that warms me instantly and her delicious *beef bourguignon*[5], I begin my story between two bites of beef and trying not to omit anything in my speech. When my story is over, she changes her face and says to me:

— But, Veronique, tell me, what happened? I had no more news from you. Why haven't you come home, don't you remember the way? Have you been sequestered? You know, I never moved because I was sure you would come back someday. A mom feels these things, thank you Lord, it's a real miracle.

I'm really annoyed by this situation, not daring to upset her. I listen calmly and enjoy this evening. However, she confuses me with me for her daughter, I tell myself that it is not important, since I intend to leave the next morning. Selfishly, I choose

---

[5] Traditional dish of Burgundy cuisine, cooked in red wine

to spend my night in the warmth.

My company this evening is pleasant to her and it makes her feel good. She offers me once again to stay this evening. So, I accept with pleasure. She smiles at me.

We spend the whole evening Talking about anything and everything, when I realized that I was dozing off, I got up and went to bed.

The next morning, I wake up with a start, I don't know where I'm and suddenly, I remember. "*My god, it's past eleven o'clock*", I said aloud. I ruffle my hair and go to the kitchen, hoping to find Mrs. Blin. She is there over tea, watches me slowly move forward and smiles at me.

I apologize for the late hour. She offers me breakfast and I sit down next to her.

So, my darling, did you sleep well? What would you like to drink this morning? I'm so happy to finally see you again, if you only knew.

— Hello, I want some cup of tea, thank you. Uh!! I have to talk to you, thank you again for your hospitality, but I have to leave right after I drink my tea, I told her softly.

Her face turns pale and her eyes instantly change color, I can see anger there. She scares me. I don't know what to do or what to say. All of a sudden, she gets up, approaches me quickly, grabs me by the arm and leads me into the bedroom, shouting:

— Veronique, what's going on my baby? Why do you want to leave? I'm your mother. Don't you want to stay with me?

You are not going to abandon me anymore.

She takes me to her daughter's room, pushes me onto the bed and double-locks the door. I'm stunned, I really didn't think she would do this. I try to think quickly because I absolutely have to get out of this apartment. I call her through the door and ask her to open it, promising not to leave not to leave.

Long after, I hear the sound of the key in the lock, she opens the door slowly and places on the desk, without a word, a tray of food and a cup of tea I'm sitting on the bed and not moving. I thank her, she comes out and locks the door. I just understood that this is going to be complicated, I must not take it head-on, but on the contrary soften it up and get into the game if I want to get out of it.

I'm hungry, I sit at the desk, eat and drink the tea. Half an hour later, my head is spinning, I feel stoned and lethargic. She must have drugged my tea.

I wake up at the end of the afternoon, it is almost dark. I notice that the meal tray has been cleared. I'm not feeling well, I'm nauseous, I call her through the door and ask her permission to use the bathroom. She comes into the bedroom and accompanies me; I can hardly walk. She looks at me tenderly and says:

— Look at what you make me do Veronique, why do you want to leave me already when we have barely found each other, I don't understand. You remember when you were little you never wanted me to be far from you. You were gripping my legs. My baby, tell me you remember that, and please don't leave me again, the last time our separation was too hard.

— Do not worry. I promise to stay with you Mom, I tell her, lying.

— It's fine my dear, now go get some rest, you're still tired, I'm going to cook us a good meal for tonight. Go to sleep my baby, she said, placing a light kiss on my forehead.

I go back to the bedroom, lie down and hear the door closing and the sound of the key in the lock.

Time goes by, she only agrees to take me out of the room for a quick shower and a meal tray, tells me stories of my "so-called" childhood while smiling, sometimes she laughs and constantly says "*Do you remember my baby?*"

She makes me really sad; I have the impression that she is a nice woman, but that the pain has just made her lose her mind. I'm so sorry for her. So, I stay calm knowing that she won't hurt me.

I don't know how long I've been locked in this room, because every day is the same and I sleep almost all the time because of the drugs she puts in my drinks.

One morning, when I wake up, I see the door open, I go out slowly, leaning against the wall because I still feel nauseous. Looking around, I see her in the kitchen, sitting at the table, half in her thoughts. The sound of my footsteps makes her raise her head; she says to me:

— Christine, come close to me, please.

I sit down, surprised to be called by my first name. She gently puts her hand on my arm and confesses:

— I don't understand what happened to me the other time, I'm so sorry for what happened this holiday season makes me so wistful and nostalgic.

— And then seeing you wearing Veronique's clothes brought back so many memories in me that I lost track of time and control of myself. I'm sorry if I scared you and also locked you up in her room.

It's Christmas Eve tomorrow, please forgive me, I'm going to explain, tell you everything about my daughter, I thought about it all night, I brooded over all the things of this painful memory, turned them in all directions. Even though it's unforgivable what I did to you, please Christine tries to understand me, she begs.

She said to me casually, "*This year she would have been twenty-three*". Then she tells me about the life of her daughter

Veronique, her sufferings, her sorrows and the joys they lived together. I remain speechless, I want to know what happened to Veronique, but I resign myself not to ask her, I'm afraid to awaken in her more sadness than she already has, bad memories. I'm stuck, I can't speak anymore. A long silence settles between us, she closes her eyes, I hardly dare to breathe, for fear of disturbing her in her memories.

I know she's kidnapped me, but I feel her so fragile, and ultimately, she's nice to me. This outstretched hand that she did not hesitate to offer me, I can, I want to forgive her for her gesture. Ten minutes later, Marie-Claude opens her eyes and finally tells me:

Three years ago, she killed herself. However, nothing showed any pain in her.

I didn't understand her gesture, I didn't see it coming and one morning I found her in the tub, immersed in her blood, both wrists cut off. I called her, yelled her name trying to wake her up, but it was too late, she was already gone, without a letter, without an explanation, she told me, bursting into tears.

I want to hug her to comfort her, but I dare not. For a moment, I have the feeling that, in fact, it's me who wants to be hugged. Everything is confused, I stay in my place very moved.

She explains to me that for a long time her daughter's friends met at her house, that she needed to hear about her daughter Veronique, to hear the stories of her life with her friends, to learn things about her. Together, they looked at pictures of her as a child and videos from her vacation. After a while, the visits faded.

Now, most of the time, she is alone, facing herself. My company is pleasant to her and does her good. She suggests that I spend Christmas Eve and the end of the year celebrations with her. I gladly accept. She smiles at me and says calmly:

— You know, compared to what happened, I thought about it a lot and I have to talk to you seriously.

I imagine the worst in what she wants to tell me.

5.

Compassion

In Jouy-aux-Arches with my grandparents

My distraught mother talks with my grandmother.

— It's been so long now, I can't take it anymore, why the police isn't advancing, and why did I slap her? I didn't realize that I'm asking her too much.

— It's high time you noticed, said my

grandmother, angry with my mother, "I told you, you know Christine is talking to me and it's not easy for her, she thinks you prefer Marie. Especially since we no longer do anything with it. You rely on Christine rather than your husband. Your daughters must spend the same amount of time with their mother. Just because you see her tall doesn't mean she doesn't need attention and hugs It's difficult for young teenagers these days. You are losing her, my poor girl.

— But you think it's easy for me! When I was a teenager, you weren't particularly nice to me and in every sense of the word. I got out of it without too much trouble, I'm not dead, she said, raising her voice.

— It was not the same time Lucie; you have to live with your times my daughter. I admit being closer to my granddaughters,

I'm surely more of a grandmother than I was a mother to you at the time, but you did not have the same concerns. Please lower your tone, that won't make her come back any faster.

Paris

Sitting opposite Marie-Claude Blin, I say nothing, and observe her.

— I thought a lot last night Christine, this situation, well your situation and I said that because I put myself in your parents' shoes, the anguish they must be feeling right now. I think you should call them.

— No, I'm too angry with them, and then that wouldn't change a thing because it is out of the question that I will return to them. Frankly I think they're happier without me, I said, lowering my head.

— I do not believe, you react as an

angry young girl, currently you are angry and I think a little lost too, but one day you will be a mother too and you will understand things differently.

— Maybe…

— I can no longer hold my daughter in my arms nor can I console her or hug her when she is sad, or share a good laugh with her like we used to. She's gone forever, to a better world, although I would have preferred that better world to be by my side. I miss her so much if you only knew. I can feel what your mom must be feeling right now. Don't be too hard on her, on them, adult life is not easy you know, she said, stroking my cheek and searching my eyes. I'm not telling you this to bother you Christine, think about it anyway, please. You can stay here as long as you want, as I wouldn't be reassured to know you outside in this cold, think about what I told you, weigh the pros and cons. Sometimes we have to face things, even if it hurts.

— Thank you very much, but I think it would be better for me if I left your flat, I told her coldly.

I immediately regret the coldness of my voice, because she does not deserve it. I'm completely upset by her words. I'm mentally tired, and psychologically exhausted. What if she was right? And if I hadn't run away, how would my return home have been? So many questions jostle in my head.

I think of a possible return, but I'm afraid, afraid of my parents' reaction, that my mother does not understand me, afraid that she will push me away. I'm also afraid my dad will be mad at me.

On the other hand, I miss Marie my little

sister. My grandparents and my family must be so worried.

We didn't longer talk about it again. Despite the concern to transfer that Mrs. Blin had do on me concerning her daughter and my afraid of the moment, I decided to stay at her place for Christmas Eve and the end of the year, I forgave her because I feel really good with her.

I know it might sound weird, having been kidnapped. I was really very scared, but yet I feel sympathy and empathy for her, I understand her suffering because I am suffering too. Besides, it's not her fault, her pain is too great.

We get along very well, she talks to me with respect about anything and everything like an adult, not like my mother who doesn't think I'm responsible, and leans on me constantly.

So, I did not leave Mrs. Blin, nor go out in the days following our conversation. We spend the end of the year celebrations together in joy and good humor, she gave me gifts, which was very nice of her. I help her here and there with the chores, we cook together. We have fun together; I feel comfortable with her as if we were family and I live again a little.

Suddenly, in the middle of the afternoon of Tuesday 4th January 1983, the doorbell rang and I was startled. Marie-Claude gets up and notices my anguish, but says nothing and goes to the entrance of the flat.

She opens the door, talks to the people in the doorway, I can't hear what they are saying. Then she comes back, but she is not alone. Next to her, three police officers in uniform: a tall man in his thirties with jet-black hair cut very short, a piercing gaze, and two women in their forties with brown hair tied in a ponytail, come towards me smiling. They explain to me in a soft voice that I have to follow them to the police station, then my parents will come and get me. I scream, I don't want to go with them, I beg Mrs. Blin to keep me with her. I'm furious, I'm desperate.

I don't understand why she's doing this to me. We're good together! I've even forgiven her for my lockdown, I really don't understand why she's doing this to me. I'm lost. Seeing that I have no choice, I collect my things and leave the flat. Marie-Claude explains to me that I will understand later, but that she has no choice, I'm an underage and it is for my own good.

I leave with the police officers under

duress, sad and without a word to Mrs. Blin, I'm devastated and I feel betrayed by the only person I thought had become a friend.

6.

Upheaval

I wait in a small room waiting for my parents to arrive, they have been warned. A few hours later, I hear a noise in the corridor, two men are talking, but I can't hear what they are saying. I think I recognize daddy's voice, then I see him, he's with one of the police officers, he is wearing his gray suit, the same one he wears when he comes home from work on Friday nights. My heart leaps, it's adrenaline, fear and joy mixed together. He is happy to see me again and smiles. I look for my mother behind him, she's not there, she probably didn't want to come. He is indeed alone, he approaches me, draws me towards him and hugs me. He kisses me tenderly on the cheek. I burst into tears and hug him tightly, to make the most of this hug with him, and instantly, I ask for forgiveness.

He reassures me by calmly telling me that we will discuss it later, that I had nothing to worry about. He settles the last formalities with the police and we leave. As it was night, Dad explained that we were going to sleep in a hotel in Paris and that we would leave very early the next morning. I'm happy, I have my father all to myself like before. So, I savor this moment.

He tries to make me understand the

sorrow that my running away has caused around me, Marie says that it's her fault. That he had to reassure my grandparents, my cousins, my aunts, saying that the whole family was in turmoil. Dad tells me that it was really selfish of me to run away, that I should have called him and told him what was going on at home, that we could have talked about it during the weekend.

You can imagine our anguish; we have been looking for you for a month. If that person you were staying with hadn't called the police station. My God, I don't even dare to think about it.

The next day, very early in the morning, we set off for home. I'm terribly anxious, even though the talk with my father went relatively well, I'm afraid of the meeting with Mum. I hardly say anything on the way home, I even pretend to be asleep at

71

times so I don't have to talk to her.

But my head is full of questions, I try to imagine the meeting with my mother and I'm afraid, something has broken between me and her, at least for me, and I don't know how to get back to her. But is it really up to me to come back, to take the first step? All these unanswered questions finally make me fall into a deep and restful sleep.

The moment I didn't want arrives, I have a lump in my throat and my stomach hurts like crazy, my dad drives the car into the driveway. I see Marie smiling outside the window. My father explains that she refused to go to school because she wanted to wait for me. I walk through the door looking at the ground, Marie jumps into my arms and I hold her tenderly. She cries and asks me to forgive her for taking and soiling my school things. I hug her tightly and tell her:

— Don't worry, it's not your fault, my sweety.

My mother is two meters away from me and stares at me, I meet her gaze, but I refuse to take the first step towards her. Without moving, Mum holds out her arms to me. A few minutes later, not seeing me move, she walks over to me and draws me against her. I cried without a word coming out of my mouth and huddled in my mother's arms.

— I've made you a birthday lunch for this lunchtime, I know it was your birthday a fortnight ago, you know the festive season without you has been really difficult, so I asked your grandparents to come today. Are you happy? my mother asks me half-heartedly.

— Yes, thanks Mum, I say with a smile.

I go up to my bedroom to change. I stay there for a while; I hear a soft knock on the door. I say "*come in*" and I see a tiny blond girl asking me for permission to walk through my doorway, she has never asked before.

As I enter, she hands me a very colorful drawing she made for me. She climbs on my lap and tells me about her week like a chatterbox. I'm happy to spend time with my little sister, because during this special time I don't talk to my mother. Even though I suspect that it will have to come to that.

My mother calls us, my grandparents have just arrived, Marie and I go downstairs hand in hand, smiling. My grandmother, who is nicknamed Olivia because she wanted to curl her hair and turn it blonde, to look like *Olivia Newton-John* in "Grease", hugs me and tells me she is happy I'm safe. My grandfather, who is nothing like *John Travolta*, but more like *Michel Galabru*[6], as is his sense of humor, kisses me and tells me that I have lost a lot of weight.

I sit next to them, I'm happy to see them, happy that things are finally going well. We chat, we laugh at my grandfather's jokes, a certified professional to lighten the family atmosphere.

The improvised birthday meal and the afternoon go really well. No one mentions my running away. It's very warm and I'm reliving a bit.

---

[6] French actor (1922-2016)

All in all, it's not so bad that Mrs. Blin has made arrangements for me to go home. I have the impression that nothing has happened, at least without any complications, my mother does not reproach me anything. But I haven't had any explanations with her yet. I think she's too ashamed of the violent slap she gave me.

That's it! Everyone is gone, I got many gifts from my grandparents and also from my parents. I go back to my bedroom to listen to music, Queen, Telephone, Supertramp, Falco, Peter Gabriel, Culture Club... My favorites of the moment, I feel like it's been a long time since I heard them. Lying on my bed, I savor this magical moment by reading an old Podium magazine[7] which is lying around in my

---

[7] Same magazine than "Jackie or Just Seventeen"

room.

In the evening, I ask my parents if I'm going to school the next day because I really want to see my friends again and they answer together, like a chorus:

— NO!!! We want to enjoy you a little and try to understand what happened so that it doesn't happen again.

— And then, my mother continues, we have an appointment for you in a few days, we'll talk about it tomorrow morning. Have a good night, I'll wake you up around eight o'clock. Good night, my daughter.

— Good night, Mum, thank you again for this beautiful family day.

She hugs me, kisses me and I go up to my room, anxious not to know what they want to tell me.

7.

Treason

As expected, my mother wakes me up slowly, I get ready and go downstairs to have my breakfast. Then my parents ask me to come into the living room and suggest that I sit around the table where there are papers, pamphlets like advertisements. My father hands me one, my body stiffens and begins to tremble. I look carefully at the leaflet and read what it says; Private High School Beau Jardin, under the supervision of the Christian Doctrine and boarding school for girls in Saint-Dié-des-Vosges.

Suddenly pale, I look up at my parents. I don't understand. Everything was back to normal. I wasn't even punished when I came back, on the contrary, I even had the right to a birthday meal.

Why are they doing this to me? I feel betrayed, I'm angry, I cry, I beg them not to do this, that I need them, not to take me away from them. Why don't they love me?

Finally, I realize that they don't understand me, that they don't want to know why I left. Will they really dare to send me there? I cry my eyes out, I can't believe it, I don't want to go. My father calmly explains to me that after what I did, it couldn't be otherwise, that I was gone for more than a month and that I can't imagine what they must have felt during that time, this continuous fear every day, not knowing if I was still alive, not to mention nights without sleep. And above all, that I lost their trust.

I try to open my mouth to explain myself, so that they understand. My mother cuts me off and asks me to listen to them first.

"But they don't ask me how I feel about them. They have to understand that if I left, there was a good reason. I feel like they are the only ones who matter. Where do I fit into their plan? Why don't they ask me anything and impose their will on me?"

My parents tell me that I should have thought before I acted because what I did is really very serious. I'm devastated. They talk, they talk, but they don't try to understand, they don't want to know anything, they don't ask me any questions about what I experienced in Paris. I feel a second abandonment on their part.

The rest of the week is simple, I'm grounded, I'm 'not allowed to go out with my friends, not even in front of the house. My mother explains to me that at the beginning of next week we will go to Private High School Beau Jardin to visit it and finalize the registration. Their decision is made and I can't say anything.

Saint-Dié-des-Vosges

My father drives the car into the driveway towards the front of the school. I discover a large old building lost in the middle of nowhere, filled with greenery, outside the town with a small mountain just behind it.

— Do you see how nice it is, Christine? says my mother, turning to me. The school is named after that mountain behind it, 'Beau Jardin Mountain'.

— Yeah, great! I'm glad to hear that, I say in a soft voice, not caring at all.

— It's so beautiful, Mum, says Marie.

We are greeted by a woman dressed in a black chasuble dress and white headdress, who introduces herself as the Mother Superior of this boarding school. I try to be polite and courteous, but I sulk, and she notices.

— So, Miss, what's going on? You're not very cheerful. You'll be fine here. Look at your future classmates, they don't look unhappy.

I notice some girls coming out of a classroom without speaking and I dare to ask a question, which may seem stupid, but not to me:

— There are no boys, it's not mixed?

— Uh no, it's not mixed, Miss Christine, she replies outraged.

As we walk through the corridors, the Mother Superior shows us the classrooms, the library and the gym. She explains to me in a solemn voice as we pass the refectory that the Holy Bible is read by each student in turn during the meal. She explained that the classes were almost the same as those at my old school, but with an additional one in Christian education, in order to teach us the benefits of living in a religious community.

We arrived in her office and she spoke

84

to my parents:

— Before I show you the boarding school, you have some papers to fill in, so I'm going to ask you as planned for the payments for January 1983, prorate of course, then February and March. I would also like to give you the house rules which you will have to read and sign, as well as Christine.

She hands me some stapled sheets, I read them diagonally and retain the worst for myself.

• At the Beau Jardin Private School, all our boarders must be polite.

• Complete silence in class, in the corridors and in the outdoor areas.

• We do not allow any jewelry or make-up and long hair must be tied back.

- No chewing gum is allowed on the school premises.

- All packages received must and will be shared with dorm mates.

- The average must not be less than 14, or you will be given a weekend detention.

- Inside the dormitories before curfew, we do not accept any noise, and especially no music.

- Lights out at 9 pm, morning wake up at 7 am, breakfast at 7.45 am and the first class is at 8.45 am.

- Uniforms and shoes must always be clean.

It goes on like that for almost four pages. I put the sheets on the table, take a pen and sign in disgust without even reading the rest.

We head for the boarding school, our host opens the door, I notice a room with ten beds, five on each side, a bedside table and a wardrobe, not even bedside lamps, no privacy. All the beds are made and nothing is left on the night tables, I have the impression that nobody sleeps there.

I ask her:

— There is no desk, Madam.

— You have to call me Mother and for your teachers, it's Sister; and no, a dormitory is for sleeping, so you don't need a desk. You have a study room for your homework. You will collect a uniform today before leaving and will arrive with it, on Monday 17th January, the day you start school, as there is no civilian clothing is allowed on the school premises. The second one will be in your wardrobe in case of need. Do you have any questions?

I'm so disgusted that I will soon be in this prison that I don't open my mouth, let alone in the car on the way home, despite my mother's exclamations that this place is so extraordinary. With big, stupid phrases like: "*I would have loved to study here when I was your age*". I spend my last week at my parents' house, most rotten of my life. I can't even see my friends to say goodbye. Since I ran away, I haven't even spoken to them. If they ring the doorbell, my mother tells them I'm not available. If they phone me, it's the same. My mother is there all the time, she's taken time off work for the occasion. She's always watching me, I can't even go to the local bakery to get bread, I'm never alone. All I want to do is run away again and never come back. I can't take it anymore. I have just a little respite because I spend three days at my grandparents with Marie, who doesn't let me out of her sight, as if my mother had taught her a lesson.

I try to talk to my grandmother to get her to change my parents' minds, to explain to her that it's a real prison, but nothing works.

8.

Claim

Forced and coerced, on January 17th,
1983 at 8.30 am, dressed like a clown in
that horrible uniform, I entered a prison,
taken by my executioners of parents. "*God,
if there is a god hidden within these grey
walls, release me*", I beg you. My parents
drop me off in front the entrance, kiss me,
wish me a good week and leave with a little
wave. I try to form a smile, but anyone can
see that it is forced. I turn on my heels,
dragging my suitcase for the week behind

me. I arrive at the school grounds and head for the school reception. I introduce myself; a sister calls a student dressed like me, and explains that we are in the same class, asks her, by handing her a paper, to direct me to dormitory number 2A so that I can deposit my suitcase and then orders her to take me quickly to see Sister Marie-Audrey of the library, in order to pick up my books and notebooks.

— Hello, my name is Sylvie Decaux, you can follow me Miss.

I see a girl a little taller than me, really pale with freckles all over her face, her dark red hair pulled back impeccably with a big black velvet elastic. I think she has a certain charm. Her voice is very soft, like that of a young child. I look her straight in the eye and answer:

— Christine, my name is Christine

Sogera, this is my first day here.

— Follow me, please, we'll walk fast because classes start at 8.45 am.

— Ok, I said softly as I hurried along. Excuse me Sylvie, how long have you been a student here?

— Don't worry, it'll come to you on its own. I'm starting my second year.

— Have you been punished too?

— No, Christine, my parents wanted me to continue my studies here and I accepted, I live in Nancy and my parents are often away, so it's obviously easier for the three of us, she continues, smiling.

— It's not too hard?

— It's actually quite strict here, but it's okay, it's not a prison either, she smiles. You'll get used to it, don't worry.

As we head out of the building, I

recognize the path to the boarding school I visited with my parents last week in the distance.

Quickly, we put my suitcase there and hurriedly left for the library. Once inside, we went to a sister to ask her for my books. When this was done, Sylvie and I hurried towards the classroom as it was 9.05am and we were already late.

Sylvie knocks on the door and we wait for the order to enter:

— Come in, orders a loud, dry voice.

— Hello, Sister Marie Dominique, says Sylvie. I apologize for the delay; I introduce Christine Sogera; she is new, I accompanied her to drop off her things at the boarding school and collect her books and notebooks.

— Very well, thank you Sylvie, I have

been warned, please sit down.

Then she turned to me and looked at me:

— Hello Miss, come to my side, turn to your classmates and introduce yourself to the class.

— Hello everyone, my name is Christine Sogera, and this is my first day, I changed schools after the Christmas holidays, before I was in Metz in a state school, I said briefly not knowing what else to say.

— Can you explain to the class why the sudden change of schools?

— No, it's none of their business, it's personal!

— Well, she replies, I think it's the class business. You should know, ladies, that your new classmate has run away from home for more than a month, putting her parents in anguish, and...

— Be quiet! I shout. Who do you think you are, exposing my personal life to everyone?

— You should have thought before acting, Miss! And lower your voice, because you risk being punished on your first day at your new school. Go and sit down at the back of the class and be quiet. I make the rules here, not you. Let's start again, open your math 'book, page six, please.

— I go and sit down, disgusted, distressed, no words could describe how I feel at the moment. I ask myself *"What on earth is this place?"* I already feel like leaving and it's only the beginning. I follow the math 'class, forced but without real attention, and I pout. The classes continue one after the other. Sylvie guides me in silence and does not dare to speak about what happened with Sister Marie-Dominique in the first class.

At mealtime, I pick at my plate, I'm not hungry. I hear the person reading the Bible in the distance and I really wonder what I'm doing here. My parents are not even religious.

I notice the Mother Superior in the distance, I think she is making her rounds, unfortunately she comes up to me and looks at my almost full plate while the other girls are already eating their dessert.

— Hurry up and finish! she orders.

— I'm not hungry and it's disgusting, I say, glaring at her.

— Excuse me, Miss, I heard you. Do you know that there are people starving in the world?

— That's their problem, not mine, I said cheekily.

— Well, it's not starting well with you. You've been here since this morning and you are already, showing off. Get up and come with me to my office immediately, she insists.

— But....

— I said get up and follow me to my office, she said, grabbing my arm and pulling me towards her.

— I follow her, crying with rage under the mocking looks of the girls and the worried look of Sylvie.

— When I arrive at her office, she explains the rules once again, telling me that I have read and signed the rules of procedure, so that I'm aware of the sanctions in case of bad behaviour on my part. She talks to me, but I don't really care for I 've decided that I'm going to do everything to get kicked out anyway.

— As punishment, I have a six-page essay on "World Famine" due in two days and by 6pm. Seriously, it's a load of rubbish. I'm not doing it, it's out of the question. After a while they'll get so fed up with me that they'll send me home. My parents will have to send me back to my old school.

The first night in this impersonal dormitory is catastrophic, I hardly sleep at all. Too much noise, too much light coming through the shutters. Girls tossing and turning in their beds, not to mention snoring and talking in their sleep. The next morning I'm extremely pissed off because I'm tired, and I complaint all the time. In class I don't participate, I don't even work. I'm fed up!

In the corridors between classes, I meet the mother superior who reminds me of the essay I have to do and tells me that I can find all the books I need in the library. I give her a "*yes, yes Mother*", knowing full well that I won't do it.

Wednesday arrives, it's almost half past five. I haven't even started, I've gone to the library to be alone and quiet, and I've just taken the opportunity to write letters to my friends at my old school, to try to explain to them what I'm going through here, what my parents dared to do, and especially that I'll soon be coming back to them.

At the appointed time, I pretended to have forgotten, but the Mother Superior summoned me to her office.

— I'll take your essay. How did it go? It wasn't too hard; did you find all the information you needed to do it?

— I haven't done anything and I don't intend to do it.

I want to get out of here and go home quickly, I say, sure of myself!

— Excuse me ?!, she says, taken aback by my words and my cheeky look. So, Miss Sogera, I've already got negative feedback from your teachers, you're not doing anything in class, what's going on?

Suddenly she softens her voice and says to me:

— Talk to me Christine, I'm not your enemy. You may not know it, but we have a confessional here in the chapel. It's anonymous and confidential, you can talk without being judged and we can also counsel you. I think that would do you a lot of good. I understand you, you know, and I know that this situation is not easy for you, you may not realize why you are here, and you have lots of questions. You want to talk about why you ran away? You know Christine, I was young too. I didn't have my vocation to God from birth, it started after my teenage years. Listen to me, as you've just arrived, I'm going to give you a second chance and you'll have to hand in this essay in a week, but be careful Christine, you won't get a third chance. Do we agree?

I nod, thank her and leave her office. I like her idea of a confessional and it makes me think a lot. It's true that I've been through so much, between the anger towards my mother, the runaway, the sexual assault I suffered and also the confinement in Paris. I buried all that in a box in the back of my brain locked up, and I forgave my detractors. But have I really forgiven myself? Have I really forgotten? I'm not closing the door to confession, not for my sins, but rather for my suffering.

I go back to Sylvie in the study room and tell her what the Mother Superior told me. Sylvie explains to me that in this school there is a good relationship between the students and the adults in the staff members.

So, why not take advantage of this to try and win them over and do what I want to do, which is to leave the school and go home.

I try to participate in class as best I can, because I give on one side and take away on the other; but I always refuse to do the essay given as a punishment by the Mother Superior.

9.

Confidences

I head to the chapel in question, it's 5.30 pm and I figured out that it wasn't too crowded at that hour. I walk in and notice a confessional with two doors, just like in the movies I have seen, having never been in a church before with my parents. I've been thinking a lot and I feel the need to talk to try and understand this rage and pain I feel inside me. I feel so lost. I enter the closed confession booth, close the door and wait. There is a dividing door, but there is no one on the other side. I hesitate to stay, and just as I put my hand on the handle to leave, I hear talking on the other side of the barrier.

— I'm listening, my child, says an unknown voice.

— I don't know what to do in this place.

— Just tell me what you want, what's on your mind, a soft female voice reply.

I jump in with confidence because she doesn't know who I am.

— Well, I've been in a kind of a whirlwind of thinking lately and I've been asking myself many questions on a lot of different subjects. I don't know how long I can stay chatting with you, so I'll talk about what hurts me the most.

— I'm listening to you.

— It's quite embarrassing.

— Don't worry, I can hear everything and it will remain between us, it's confidential.

— So, I'm going for it! I was raped a while ago, I forgave the boy, because I thought it would be enough to forget, but I have a lot of nightmares about it now and everything is confused in my head. I feel so dirty, I know it's my fault because I shouldn't have agreed to let him kiss me, it all happened so fast.

I talk to her; explain my pain and I cry because everything has come back to the surface. And then the woman on the other side consoles me with soothing words and tells me things that call out to me and reassure me all at once.

— It's not your fault my child, he had no right, you are a victim, you had great courage to come and confide in me. I am proud of you. Your anger is legitimate you know, know that you are not alone. You can come and talk to me every day if you wish.

— Thank you very much, Madam.

— Have you met a doctor?

— No, I haven't even talked to my parents about it, you're the first person I've dared to talk to about it.

— If you want, you can talk to the school nurse, she can direct you...

— No, no, I don't want this to get out, I'm too ashamed, even though I know now that it's not my fault.

— Don't worry, you can decide when you are ready.

— Thank you so much for listening to me, I feel a bit better now.

I quickly leave the confession booth, to make sure that the person does not know who I am.

I come back to talk to her almost every night of the week after the study, it makes me feel better, Mother Superior was right. But the more time passes, the more I want to leave this school, I don't belong here. In fact, I don't even know where I belong.

It's time to hand in the essay on "World Famine", I've only done one page instead of the six required, and it's rather sloppy, but at least I've done a bit. The Mother Superior is really not happy, and tells me straight away:

— I'm going to tell your parents that you're sanctioned for the weekend.

— What does that mean? said I, looking even more cheeky.

— It's simple Miss Christine, you're staying at school, so you're not going home this Friday. That's it!

I yell at her that it's out of the question.

— You can't stop me, you were nice last week, that's why I made the effort. Besides, I went to the confessional too. In fact, you say you're helping me, but you stab me in the back like my parents.

— Calm down, Miss, you know, we've tamed worse ones than you, she says.

And then everything changes, I scream, I cry, I run in the corridors, I'm completely lost, I feel like I'm crazy. I have a nervous breakdown, I feel arms blocking me, I struggle and try to run away, but I feel a sting in my shoulder. And then it's a total blackout.

I wake up in an almost white room, with two beds side by side, I'm completely disoriented and anxious, my stomach cramps. I think I'm in the school infirmary, I notice a sister approaching me, she asks me how I feel, offers me a soup, telling me that I'll stay there for the night to rest as much as possible, explains that I've had an emotional shock and that I've been given an injection to calm me down because I could have hurt myself.

Sylvie came to visit me very briefly, but it didn't soothe me to see her. I'm too stressed about not being able to go home that weekend.

When I get up the next morning, I ask the nurse if she told my parents about my seizure the day before.

— Yes, she confirms.

— Will they come and get me? say I, feeling confident.

— Not that I know of, and then you're fine now, aren't you? Your classmate Sylvie has been called, she'll come and get you and you can go and wash up and get ready for the day's lessons. In the meantime, I've brought you breakfast.

I'm speechless, stunned by what I have just heard, and deep inside I think that my parents no longer care about me. I experience this as yet another abandonment.

10.

Release

Meanwhile, in Corny-sur-Moselle

— I'm really worried, my father said to my mother. Aren't we going too far with Christine? She had a nervous breakdown yesterday, and this weekend she's being punished and she won't be coming home.

— I'm afraid she'll run away again.

— Would you please stop it, James, she has to understand and follow the rules, what she did to us was very serious? Have you already forgotten? If we give in now, she'll do as she pleases. You agreed to this. Don't go back on your decision, darling. You'll see in ten days, when she comes back on her next weekend, she'll be happy and everything will be fine, says my mother.

— Yes, I know, said my father. But still, I've never seen you so hard before, she's a nice kid you know, it's the first time she's done something like that. And sorry but, if instead of slapping her once more you would have asked the reason why she did what she did. And above all if you would have explained your action, we wouldn't be dealing with this right now. You're also overprotective of Marie. Look, you offer her goldfish because she misses her sister, is that serious? You...

— I can't believe it! You're blaming

me now, my mother yells. What do you know? You're never here, always on the road. I'm always alone with the girls, sometimes I feel like I'm single. Ah, that's a nice life for you, evenings in a hotel-rooms with who knows who else!

— Don't start again, I've never cheated on you.

My father gets up.

— And if it's to hear that, I'd rather go out and get some fresh air, he says, leaving the house and slamming the door.

Speeding towards his car and starting off with a bang, he hears words in the distance without really understanding what my mother is saying, who continues to shout in his direction, crying.

Private High School Beau Jardin

I beg Sylvie to understand me, to feel my confusion.

— I can't take it anymore, you have to help me, I want to get out of here.

— Don't think about it Christine, if I get caught or even you. Imagine what the Mother Superior would say, not to mention the reprisals. It's the disciplinary council all over again.

— Please don't leave me too.

— No, Christine, she said. I'm sorry.

I understand, but I'm disappointed. Why is everyone against me? I can't take it anymore. Why doesn't anyone understand me?

The next day I asked to phone my parents. They refused my request, telling me to write them a letter instead, that sometimes-putting words down on paper allows us to think better and not say things we might regret by speaking too quickly. Proofreading also allows us to understand correctly the whys and wherefores of our requests.

Sylvie tells me not to worry about my mail, and that it is sent every other day. The next departure is on Friday morning, the day after my request.

I start writing the letter to my parents. Several times I start again, I change whole paragraphs, rewrite them, I want to make it clear, I want them to understand why I want to leave this school. Why I feel so bad.

Writing calms me down a bit, unless it's the nervous exhaustion of the last few days.

I put my letter in the box provided. By depositing it, I feel a little stressed, but I'm glad I wrote it and especially because I have a new project for tomorrow and I don't need Sylvie to make it happen.

Friday 28th January 1983, I get up with a smile on my face, get ready and go downstairs to have breakfast in the quiet.

Sylvie looks at me and wonders why I have such a change of mood, she even pays me a compliment, saying that the night must have been good for me and that she is really happy for me.

The classes go well, I participate in the oral exams. The Sisters of the different subjects congratulate me. It was a perfect day for them.

At last, the end of the week's classes arrives, the time of departure, the perfect moment for my plan? I see a group of smiling students with their suitcases, heading towards their parents' cars, others towards the regional bus stop for the different destinations.

I take advantage of the horde of girls to slip between them towards the exit.

A Sister stops me at the door:

— It seems to me that you are staying here this weekend.

Having stuffed the minimum, I need into my pockets, I answer her with a big smile:

— Yes, yes, I know! Look Sister, I don't have a suitcase, I just want to accompany a friend to her bus to wish her a good weekend and get some fresh air.

She inspects me from head to toe and seeing me without a bag, lets me through and asks me not to be too long, because I must then go to the study room, where Sister Marie-Dominique, who is on through for the next two days, must explain to me and to the other students who are staying, the organization of the weekend.

I give her a "*yes*" that I think is as sincere as possible and rush out into the cold.

I look at the regional buses from a distance, they're a bit far away from the school which is perfect for me.

I walk away from the school, mingling with the other girls, trying to be natural.

I spot a bus to *Nancy*[8], I try to get on, a

---

[8] City located in the East of France

woman's voice calls out to me, it's the sister from the entrance who spoke to me earlier. She has been following me for a while without me noticing her.

I'm afraid, I don't want my plan to fail, not so close. I run, I run as fast as I can between the buses. The people around me look at me without understanding. The sister shouts at them:

— Catch her, please!

Hearing this, I cross the road without looking, like a madwoman. My heart is pounding. At that very moment, a car arrives on my right, the driver notices me and with a squeal of tires, avoids me by a hair. I get into his car and sit on the empty seat next to him, saying that there is an emergency and that I absolutely have to go to Nancy.

He still doesn't understand how I ended up in his car. With his shaggy, ash-blond, unshaven and awake hair, the man in his forties looks at me in a daze. He is still in shock from almost running me over.

No longer himself and sensing in my voice the urgency of a possible danger, he storms off without asking.

I thank him warmly, telling him he is saving my life, and ask him if he can drop me off at Nancy station. I look so distraught that he accepts without thinking. After an hour, the driver drops me off at the railway station and wishes me good luck. I wave to him as I leave.

Later, I stand in front of the train schedule board, looking for the one to Paris. As soon as I spot it, I head for track 17 and try to sneak in. Not having any money on me this time, I'm forced to dodge the fare.

Private High School Beau Jardin in Saint-Dié-des-Vosges

The Mother Superior, distraught, having learned of my escape, informed the police and my parents.

Corny-sur-Moselle - 29th January 1983

— Mummy, the postman is dropping the mail in the box, says Marie who is looking out of the window.

My mother, devastated by the news that I had run away for the second time the night before and not having slept all night, not knowing when I would be found, went like a zombie to the letterbox.

She mechanically looks at the contents

and screams when she sees one letter in particular because she recognizes my handwriting.

She runs back inside, crying to my father, who has been livid since the day before and is sitting stoically in his chair.

He is irritated and angry with my mother, having shouted at her the day before that everything was her fault.

Mum, afraid of the content of this letter, hands him the envelope, trembling.

She sits down beside him and waits. Dad quickly tore the envelope open and took out the letter, which he read aloud, trembling.

***

Private High School "Beau Jardin",

Thursday 27th January 1983

Dear Parents,

I wanted to phone you this Thursday evening ....

Yes, I wanted to call you to come and get me, I desired to explain to you why I wanted to leave this school, but the sisters refused. They said I should try to write to you instead.

I have written this letter a hundred times. I want you to understand why I ran away at the beginning of December, and I want to apologize for doing so. But I felt I had to. It was inevitable for me. I'm so angry against you, if you only knew.

Mum, I didn't understand why you slapped me so hard, I know you don't have an easy life, but that's no reason to let me do all the chores, you're the adult not me. I'm supposed to rely on you, not the other way around. That's not my role!

I don't have an easy life either, I had little problems in the previous school with some people. I never discussed it with you because it's very difficult to talk to you at the moment, and I don't understand why.

I'm sorry I lost my patience with Marie; you know I love her. It was probably an off day. Please, why didn't you come to my room to talk to me, to explain, to hug me?

You know Mum I miss your arms; I miss your hugs, I miss our chats, I miss our word games. I need you Mummy!!! I feel abandoned emotionally, teenagerhood is a time when a daughter needs her mother greatly. I need you and I need to have quality time with you.

Daddy, I'm also angry with you, because you agreed to let Mum lock me up in this boarding school, I know it was her idea, I know you would never have agreed, but you probably feel guilty because of your absences during the week, I'm sure that things are not good between you anymore.

I think you love me, even though you haven't shown it to me for a very long time, but I can't take this lack of affection anymore. I want you to know that I need to find myself in order to forgive you, because I suffer from your betrayal for having locked me up within these walls.

I can no longer stay in this prison that is the boarding school where I'm, it is not my place, my place is in my old school with my friends.

Regarding my December runaway, I want to tell you that it was really not easy for me, I was raped. To dare to write it to you is already very hard, so imagine if I had admitted it to your face. It would have been a shock for you, as well as for me. I thought I'd got away with forgiving the boy who did it, but I feel too dirty and too bad about it. I know now that it's not my fault, but I have to try to live with this pain anyway.

I was also kidnapped and drugged without my knowledge.

I had so much to tell you when I first

came home. You never asked me anything or let me talk to you. You didn't want to know what really happened while I was away, in fact you didn't even offer to take me to a doctor, to see if everything was ok.

A boy raped me Mum, maybe I'm even pregnant and I'm scared.

But none of that mattered to you, you just needed to get some kind of revenge because your nights were "disturbed" by my absence. You destroyed my existence by locking me up in this boarding school. I feel like a prisoner who has not committed any crime. I don't belong here!

Well, I want you to know that you have failed. I hate you very much for this, just as much as I hate myself.

By the time you read these words, I will be gone. Please don't look for me this time, I have too much anger in me against you. Too much distress and pain, I don't know where I stand anymore. Who am I really!

I'm in turmoil, uprooted, detached from you and the world around me! I need to sort this out on my own.

If I decide to return one day, and only then, I would like you to let me live with Grandma and Grandpa, at least they understand me. We have talked many times in the past, they don't judge me and they don't make any difference between Marie and me.

Ask them to forgive me and tell them that I love them.

Please, don't be impatient, and let me slowly put myself back together.

Your daughter Christine

11.

Renaissance

Uzès

I feel home in this charming, historic little town in the south of France. It's really beautiful, I've been told it dates back to the Renaissance and the Middle Ages. There are lovely pedestrian streets, and a beautiful main square, "*la Place aux Herbes*" where the market is held every Wednesday and Saturday.

She has bought a picturesque house in this beautiful area, not far from the square.

It's a sunny Saturday morning on the market of Uzès[9]. I walk through the aisles, twirling from one stall to another where colors, smells and flavours abound, I'm attracted by the aroma of the spices, and find this place very friendly and pleasant. I head towards the organic vegetable stall while pushing Rose in her stroller, my six-month-old daughter.

There are many people in this village of 7500 souls. Everyone wanted to enjoy the sunshine despite the dry cold of this month of March 1984, which is understandable. I was a little late joining her at the market. Taking care of a baby takes time. I love this special time I have with my daughter and I must admit I enjoy it. Everything is so Zen

---

[9] City located in the South of France

at home. I look everywhere for her; she can't be far away.

Normally, she always has the same spot on the market, she decided to start selling organic olive oils since our arrival. She has created a panel of small independent producers around her who have put their trust in her, and they have been right. She excels behind her stall, she is also very fulfilled, I'm really proud of her evolution. I turn to my daughter Rose and ask her:

— But where is Grandma hiding, dear?

She answers me with chirps that only I, her mum, can understand. Then I see her giving change to a customer, she looks up at us and smiles instantly at me as we arrive. I take Rose out of her stroller and put her in her arms. Marie-Claude kisses her tenderly on the cheek, then turns happily to the queue of customers and says:

— This is my granddaughter Rose and my daughter Christine.

I feel so at home with her and in this little town since we arrived a year ago. I think I needed this to get my life back, to rebuild myself. I managed to take my life back little by little, putting my past behind me.

Maybe one day I will come back to Corny-sur-Moselle.

But for the moment, I want to live in the present with Rose and Marie-Claude, I'm very happy. I see a therapist once a week to learn how to manage my emotions and my fears, which are unfortunately still present. I'm continuing my studies by correspondence and I hope to obtain my A-

Level degree soon.

Being a mother is a wonderful gift, my daughter Rose, with her beautiful bottle green eyes, fills me with happiness and makes me feel so serene; she may not have a daddy, but she has a family, we are her family.

Paris, one year earlier...

I've been hanging out and begging in the streets and the metro of Paris for two months now. I'm tired of it all, finding a place on the street is not easy in itself, I'm afraid of everyone, especially people like me. I refuse to talk to other young people, not wanting my last experience to happen again. I'm alone and this allows me to reflect. Sometimes, in the evening, I meet the homeless assistance association and its volunteers who give me a hot soup and also clothes. I talk to them about everything, but I lie to them about my age so that they leave me alone.

I'm so exhausted, I'm nauseous in the morning, I vomit a lot, and it's been almost four months since I last had my period. I know what that means.

Psychologically and mentally exhausted, I decide to find Marie-Claude who so kindly welcomed me a few months ago.

As I arrive in her street, I notice a big truck in front of the building, I take advantage of the movers' passage to sneak inside.

When I get to her floor, I see the front door wide open, I don't understand why.

I can hear her voice, grumbling at a tall,

bald man of almost one meter ninety:

— But be careful, this furniture is very fragile. You...

Suddenly she stops talking, she sees me in the doorway. Our eyes meet, she hesitates to come towards me, I don't think she really recognizes me, I have lost so much weight and am in such poor physical condition.

I take a step in her direction, wait a little, then finally walk slowly towards her. Tears stream down our faces. She holds out her arms to me, I run to snuggle up to her, and beg:

— It's me! I've come back and I don't want to leave, keep me with you.

— Come in, my sweety, come in.

She hugs me tightly and kisses me

tenderly. Then she steps back, looks at me and notices that I'm pregnant and that my belly is already very round.

She explains that she is moving to the south of France, to Uzès, that her Paris flat is sold.

My last visit had made her think a lot, she had changed her mind and realizing that she wanted to start her life again from scratch. She said she had to move on to live, rather than dwell on her painful past and try to survive.

— It is a sign, Christine, that you are here now. That is why, if you wish, I offer to take you there with me. I promise to take good care of you, of the baby, she said, putting her hand on my belly.

— Thank you very much Marie-Claude, I am very touched by the attention you are giving me, I said, giving her a big hug.

My baby gave her first cry on 12th September 1983 in Nimes and weighed three kilos four hundred. Her name is Rose Veronique Sogera, born of an unknown father. I am the happiest of teenagers.

Thank you, Life!

Acknowledgements

➢ Thank you so much my daughters Elodie and Laura for your patience and your first impressions. Thank you also my sons, Adrien and François for constantly supporting me in everything I do.

➢ Thank you, Valerie A. and Charazad A., for all the time spent on the English correction and especially for your valuable advice. Thank you for being my friends.

➢ I especially don't want to forget my granddaughter, Jade. Thank you for your unconditional love.

Thank you for believing in me!

144

Printed in Great Britain
by Amazon